The Snowy Day

Edited by Jenny Tyler and Gillian Doherty

First published in 2005 by Usborne Publishing Ltd, 83-85 Saffron Hill, London EC1N 8RT, England.
www.usborne.com. Copyright © 2005 Usborne Publishing Ltd.
First published in America in 2005. Printed in Dubai.

The Snowy Day

Anna Milbourne

Illustrated by Elena Temporin

Designed by Nicola Butler

Have you ever wondered
what makes it snow?

Imagine a winter's afternoon. It's so cold that
your breath turns to mist-clouds in the frosty air.

High in the clouds, raindrops freeze
into icy flakes of snow.

Then softly, silently...

the snowflakes
start to fall.

Every snowflake has six points,
but each looks different from the next.

Some look like teeny-tiny flowers

and some like frosted stars.

Soon, thousands of pretty snowflakes are dancing through the night.

They settle gently on fields and trees and rooftops.

By morning, the world is hidden
beneath a white, snowy blanket.

crunch crunch crunch

Each step you take squashes the snow and leaves a footprint behind.

There's lots to do in the snow.

You can throw snowballs
or slide down hills...

or roll a little snowball along,
so it gathers more snow...

and gets bigger and bigger...

until it's too heavy to push.

If you heave a smaller snowball on top,
you can make a snowman.

Give him shiny pebble eyes
and a carrot for a nose.

Lots of animals hide away when it's cold.

But dotted through the snow
are trails of where they've been.

Follow the trails into the trees
and you'll find a quiet place.

A family of sleepy
squirrels snuggles up
in a hollow...

and nestled in a fir tree's thick branches,
a little bird is keeping warm.

The surface of the pond has frozen
to a sheet of gleaming ice.

You might wonder if
the fish are frozen too.

But they aren't. They're swimming
safely in the chilly water below.

And buried in the mud at the bottom of the pond,
two frogs are sleeping the winter away.

Later in the day,
the sun comes out and
shines brightly in the sky.

As the snow gets warmer,
it starts to melt...

and, little by little, the world begins to reappear.
Perhaps by tomorrow the snow will all be gone.

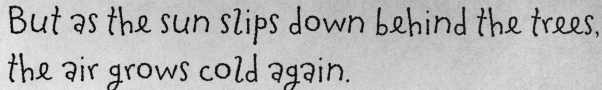

But as the sun slips down behind the trees,
the air grows cold again.

Wave goodbye
to the frosty snowman.
It's time to head for home.

In the moonlight, snowflakes whisper down once more.

They powder the ground and cover over all the footprints and trails.

The snow will melt, but not just yet.
Today is another snowy day.